ANDREW'S FAVORITE SOUPS
FOR WELLNESS AND WEIGHT-LOSS

MURIEL ANGOT
WITH ANDREW LESSMAN

PHOTOGRAPHY: LINDSEY ELTINGER
COVER PHOTOGRAPHY: TAHIA HOCKING
ASSISTANT: LOETTA EARNEST

Published by the Andrew Lessman Foundation
430 Parkson Road, Henderson, NV 89011

Printed in the United States of America.

First Printing, November 2011

ISBN 978-1-4675-0495-9

Dedicated to our mothers and grandmothers.

ABOUT THE AUTHOR

Muriel Angot was born and raised in the world's center of fine cuisine – Paris, France; however, it would take Muriel a couple of decades to rediscover her Parisian culinary roots, since she initially followed in her parents' footsteps studying Fine Art at the Sorbonne University in Paris. After college, Muriel's innate curiosity and desire to explore the world saw her leave France, spending time in Australia, Fiji, New Zealand and South America, until she fell in love with the United States where she established a beauty and wellness business in Aspen, Colorado. It wasn't until Muriel chose to attend cooking school that her true passion captured her and since that time, has never let go.

Like many French families, all the members of Muriel's family take pride in their abilities in the kitchen. But it was Muriel's paternal grandmother, Simone, who was to have the greatest influence, since she was the chef and owner of a restaurant in Picardie, France – a small city in the countryside just outside Paris. Some of Muriel's fondest childhood memories are of helping her grandmother create all the classic French dishes that were served at her restaurant. The special moments she shared with her grandmother in the culturally rich environment of an authentic French kitchen were to shape the rest of Muriel's life.

When Muriel moved from Colorado to California, the move presented an opportunity for a career change and with great trepidation she decided to take the plunge. Despite hearing how challenging and difficult it would be, Muriel followed her dream and attended Le Cordon Bleu cooking school in Paris – the same school attended by Julia Child. Ultimately, she graduated #1 in her class and now considers herself blessed to combine her two greatest passions – cooking and wellness.

FOREWORD
from Andrew Lessman

 When it comes to our health, even the best vitamins must take a backseat to the food we eat, but how does a guy who can't cook very well qualify to have his name on a cookbook? Well, I suppose that loving to eat is a good start and the fact that I know what constitutes a healthy diet is important as well, but my limited skills in the kitchen would prevent me from creating recipes you would enjoy. As a result, I have never felt qualified to write a cookbook; however, this is not really a cookbook, but my "Eating Book," since I was able to rely on a professional chef to turn my favorite foods into great recipes.

In short, the only reason this book exists is because my best friend, with whom I live, happens to be a trained professional chef. Her name is Muriel Angot and she was born and raised in Paris - the world's capital of fine cuisine and the same city where she attended the world-renowned Le Cordon Bleu cooking school made famous by Julia Child. Muriel has improved on all my favorite soups that I have enjoyed for many years and in some cases, for my entire life. It is only Muriel's exceptional talent in the kitchen that has brought all my favorite soup recipes to life and now, to you.

But why soups? Well, ever since childhood, soups have been my favorite food. They are delicious, low in calories, easy to prepare, simple to eat, easy to control portions and they enable me to enjoy many healthy foods I do not normally eat throughout the day. Soups have made it easy for me to maintain a healthy weight throughout my life, since weight control is all about portion control and since soups are liquid, there is no fooling oneself or weighing or guessing about portion size. In fact, whenever we make soups at home, we only use an 8-ounce portion and store them in the refrigerator in 8-ounce glass storage bowls. We can then simply eat them cold or reheat them in the microwave. In this way, we ensure that we never consume more than an 8-ounce cup of soup. Sadly, typical soup bowls are enormous and caloric levels skyrocket, but with an 8-ounce cup of soup your portions are always low calorie.

When you look at the recipes, you will notice that many of these soups contain beans and legumes, since they are so remarkably rich in protein and fiber, which also makes these soups healthy, hearty and filling. You will also find soups containing a wide range of healthy fruits and vegetables including of course cruciferous vegetables, along with a myriad of herbs and spices that are so rich in healthy phytonutrients. I have always included these healthy ingredients in my soups, since I have found that I often do not eat them sufficiently and soups make it so much easier for me to eat better. As a child I simply enjoyed soup, but as a busy adult, I have found that as far back as college, soups have been an easy, affordable and delicious way to eat better. I hope you feel the same way after reading our book.

Best of Health,

INTRODUCTION

This cookbook did not start as either Andrew's idea or mine, but your idea, since it is simply the result of Andrew being so frequently asked what he eats each day. I can confirm that I have heard him asked that question countless times, so I thought there might be some interest in an easy-to-follow cookbook that presents Andrew's favorite foods – his very own soups, which I can confirm, he eats daily. I had always heard Andrew talk about one day writing a cookbook that summarizes his favorite healthy foods, but he never found the time and also realized that he lacked the skills in the kitchen. So when I volunteered, he was kind enough to let me run with the idea and this book is the result.

Of course, since this book contains Andrew's soups, they are first and foremost healthy, so I had to restrain my "French" tendencies to add cream, butter and the like. Instead, I did what I could with Andrew's choice of healthy herbs and spices and I am confident you will find the results delicious. I remained faithful to Andrew's original recipes and only made changes here and there to enhance the flavor or the ease of preparation. As with any recipe, you can feel free to add your own creative touches to make them your own and I welcome any suggestions you might have. You can feel free to share them with me at my website: www.EatingWellwithMuriel.com.

Andrew always says that what we eat each day is the most important factor in our health and, not surprisingly, Andrew has always maintained an extremely healthy diet. He has never liked the standard "Food Pyramid" and rarely consumes bread, pasta, white rice, potatoes or processed foods. He prefers fish and chicken over red meat and considers legumes, nuts and seeds to be a healthy additional source of protein with the added benefits of fiber and other protective compounds. After seven years of living Andrew's dietary strategies, my health, weight and energy level have all greatly improved and I enjoy what I eat more than ever. As part of Andrew's dietary strategy, he specifically seeks foods rich in compounds that research has shown can help reduce our risk of cancer, heart disease, diabetes and other degenerative diseases. He has spent many meals explaining to me why he eats the way he eats and I have been compiling all this priceless information. Hopefully, if there is sufficient interest, I will create future books that offer Andrew's favorite dietary strategies and recipes for reducing our lifetime risk of diseases, such as cancer, heart disease and diabetes.

I have been fortunate to share the last seven years with Andrew and I feel that the information I have learned allows me to eat in a way that encourages wellness, weightloss and optimum energy. It is my goal to take all the knowledge and research at Andrew's disposal, combine them with my culinary training and experience and create the most delicious recipes for the healthiest and longest life possible.

Bon Appétit!

Muriel

CONTENTS

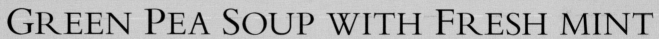

3 In a standard [ble] soup until sm[...]

GREEN PEA SOUP WITH FRESH MINT

7 CUPS • PREPARATION: 10 MINUTES • COOKING: 15 MINUTES • VERY EASY

This refreshing and hearty soup is surprisingly low in calories and extremely easy to make. This is one of the first soups I made for Andrew when he was hiking and mountain biking in Aspen a few years ago. He loves the fact that it is a rich source of protein, fiber, lutein and many other nutrients.

1 tbsp olive oil

1 medium red onion, chopped

1 clove garlic, minced

5 or 6 mini carrots, finely chopped

1 small leek, washed thoroughly and chopped

4¼ cups vegetable broth

1 pack (10 oz) frozen, organic green peas

Pinch each of salt and pepper

Mint leaves for garnish

Fresh Mint Pesto:

¾ oz fresh mint leaves

½ cup grated Parmesan cheese

2 tbsp toasted pine nuts

1 clove garlic

1 tbsp olive oil

1 tsp lemon juice

1

1 In a saucepan on
minutes until th
defrosted. Add salt an

2 Prepare the pesto
mince thorough

2

3 In a blender, purée the soup in small batches mixing for 2 to 4 minutes. Add yogurt for an extra creamy texture.

4 Serve garnished with minced mint.

Nutrition Information

Serving Size **1 Cup** Servings **8**

Calories **80**	Potassium . . . . . **155 mg**
Calories from fat . . **35**	Total Carbohydrates **10 g**
Total Fat . . . . **4 g**	Dietary Fiber . . . . . **2 g**
Cholesterol . . . . . . **0 mg**	Sugars . . . . **2 g**
Sodium . . . . **50 mg**	Protein . . . . **2 g**

Vitamin A . . . . **53 %**	Vitamin B2. . . . . **2 %**	Phosphorus. . . . . **2 %**
Vitamin C . . **319 %**	Niacin . . . . **3 %**	Magnesium. . . . . **1 %**
Calcium . . . . **2 %**	Vitamin B6. . . . **18 %**	Zinc. . . . . **2 %**
Iron . . . . **3 %**	Folic Acid. . . . **14 %**	Selenium . . . . . . **1 %**
Vitamin E. . . . . . **4 %**	Vitamin B12. . . . **1 %**	Copper. . . . . **2 %**
Vitamin B1. . . . . **3 %**	Pantothenic Acid. **1 %**	Manganese . . . . **10 %**

OTHER BENEFICIAL NUTRIENTS (PER SERVING)

Omega-3 (ALA) . . . . **47 mg**
Choline. . . . . **7 mg**
Beta-Carotene. . . . . **595 mcg**

ZUCCHINI AND HERB SOUP

5 – 6 CUPS • PREPARATION: 10 MINUTES • COOKING: 15 MINUTES • VERY EASY

This delicious, low calorie soup can be served cold in summer and is a remarkable source of lutein. The zucchini makes it very smooth and works well with all the herbs. I stir in a little bit of Greek yogurt to each serving for extra creaminess. Any yogurt will work, but I prefer the tartness of the Greek variety.

1 tbsp olive oil

1 medium yellow onion, chopped

1 clove garlic

4 zucchinis cleaned, peeled and chopped

3 cups vegetable broth

1 tbsp cumin

Pinch each of salt and pepper

1 pack (2/3 oz) fresh tarragon

Yogurt Topping:

1 cup 2% Greek yogurt

1 tsp cumin

½ tsp paprika

3 tsp fresh tarragon, chopped

Combine all ingredients until smooth and refrigerate

1 In a large saucepan over medium heat, warm the olive oil and sauté the onion, garlic and zucchini for 2 or 3 minutes until the onion becomes translucent.

2 Add the broth and bring to a boil. Add the cumin, salt and pepper. Reduce heat to low and simmer for 10 to 15 minutes until the zucchini is tender.

3 Purée in a blender or food processor until smooth.

4 Serve in individual bowls, gently mixing in a tsp of the yogurt mixture to each serving and garnishing with a sprinkle of tarragon.

Nutrition Information

Serving Size **1 Cup** — Servings **6**

Calories	86	Potassium 494 mg
Calories from fat	30	Total Carbohydrates 11 g
Total Fat	3 g	Dietary Fiber 2 g
Cholesterol	2 mg	Sugars 7 g
Sodium	115 mg	Protein 4 g

Vitamin A 13%	Vitamin B2 17%	Phosphorus 12%
Vitamin C 40%	Niacin 4%	Magnesium 9%
Calcium 11%	Vitamin B6 17%	Zinc 6%
Iron 8%	Folic Acid 12%	Selenium 3%
Vitamin E 3%	Vitamin B12 4%	Copper 5%
Vitamin K 9%	Pantothenic Acid 5%	Manganese 15%
Vitamin B1 7%		

OTHER BENEFICIAL NUTRIENTS (PER SERVING)

Omega-3 (ALA)	89 mg
Choline	20 mg
Beta-Carotene	156 mcg
Lutein & Zeaxanthin	2770 mcg

CREAM OF MUSHROOM SOUP WITH FRESH TARRAGON

8 CUPS • PREPARATION: 15 MINUTES • COOKING: 35 MINUTES • EASY

This is a meaty and earthy soup, despite being among our lowest in calories. It is rich in nutrients, including Omega-3's and can be prepared in advance and easily reheated. As with all cream soups, avoid boiling even when reheating.

1 tbsp butter

1 clove garlic

1 medium brown onion, chopped

½ cup chopped carrots

½ cup chopped celery

1 lb mushrooms (white and shiitake), chopped

2 cups water

2 cups chicken broth

¼ cup fresh tarragon, chopped

1 tbsp Sherry

4 tbsp heavy whipping cream (reserve half for optional garnish)

1 In a pot over medium heat, melt the butter gradually adding and sautéing the garlic, onion, carrots and celery. Reduce heat to low and cook for 10 minutes stirring often.

2 Add mushrooms and cook for an additional 5 minutes. Add water, broth and half the tarragon, and simmer for 20 minutes.

3 In a blender or food processor, add sherry and whipping cream mixing for a few minutes until very smooth.

4 Serve hot, garnishing with a pinch of tarragon and a mushroom cap on each bowl (tsp of cream optional).

Nutrition Information

Serving Size **1 Cup**		Servings **8**

Calories **75**		Potassium . . . . . **365 mg**
Calories from fat . . **40**		Total Carbohydrates . **6 g**
Total Fat . . . . **5 g**		Dietary Fiber . . . . . **2 g**
Cholesterol . . . . . **17 mg**		Sugars . . . . **2 g**
Sodium . . . . **55 mg**		Protein . . . . **3 g**

Vitamin A	**33 %**	Vitamin B1	**5 %**	Phosphorus	**11 %**
Vitamin C	**6 %**	Vitamin B2	**17 %**	Magnesium	**3 %**
Calcium	**3 %**	Niacin	**20 %**	Zinc	**3 %**
Iron	**5 %**	Vitamin B6	**6 %**	Selenium	**11 %**
Vitamin D3 . . .	**12 %**	Folic Acid	**5 %**	Copper	**14 %**
Vitamin E	**2 %**	Vitamin B12	**3 %**	Manganese	**11 %**
Vitamin K	**5 %**	Pantothenic Acid	**11 %**		

OTHER BENEFICIAL NUTRIENTS (PER SERVING)

Beta-Carotene	**680 mcg**
Alpha-Carotene	**278 mcg**
Lutein & Zeaxanthin	**38 mcg**
Choline	**20 mg**
Omega-3 (ALA)	**105 mg**

ONION SOUP

12 - 14 CUPS • PREPARATION: 20 MINUTES • COOKING: 1 HOUR • MEDIUM

Onions and Garlic are extremely rich sources of powerfully protective sulfur-containing compounds. I don't use croutons here, because this soup is rich and thick enough on its own and Andrew and I rarely eat bread. However, most French people would never dream of onion soup without croutons. If you decide to add the croutons, rub bread cubes with fresh garlic before putting the cheese on them (and then broil them in the oven). This improves the taste and texture tremendously.

3 tbsp olive oil

5 to 6 medium brown onions, peeled and chopped

4 cloves garlic, minced

1 tsp agave nectar

2 tbsp fresh thyme (reserve some for garnish)

1 cup dry white wine

8 cups beef broth

Salt and black pepper to taste

1 cup grated Swiss cheese

1   In a large pot over medium heat, warm the olive oil until sizzling. Add the onions sautéing and stirring regularly for 10 minutes until a golden color.

2   Add the garlic, agave and thyme stirring often. Reduce heat to low and cook for 20 minutes until the onion is dark brown – but not burned.

3 Slowly add the wine and broth, and bring to a boil. Reduce heat, cover and simmer for about 30 minutes stirring occasionally until the liquid is reduced by approximately a quarter. Add salt and pepper to taste.

4 Serve in individual bowls garnished with grated Swiss cheese and thyme.

Nutrition Information

Serving Size **1 Cup**		Servings **14**
Calories **100**		Potassium . . . . . **175 mg**
Calories from fat . . **50**		Total Carbohydrates . **5 g**
Total Fat . . . . **6 g**		Dietary Fiber . . . . . **1 g**
Cholesterol . . . . . . **8 mg**		Sugars . . . . **1 g**
Sodium . . . . **100 mg**		Protein . . . . **4 g**

Vitamin A . . . . . **2 %**	Vitamin B2 . . . . . **4 %**	Phosphorus . . . . . **9 %**
Vitamin C . . . . . **7 %**	Niacin . . . . **6 %**	Magnesium . . . . . **3 %**
Calcium . . . . . . **10 %**	Vitamin B6 . . . . **4 %**	Zinc . . . . **3 %**
Iron . . . . **3 %**	Folic Acid . . . . . **3 %**	Selenium . . . . . . **3 %**
Vitamin D3 . . . . **1 %**	Vitamin B12 . . . **4 %**	Copper . . . . **3 %**
Vitamin E . . . . . . **3 %**	Pantothenic Acid . **2 %**	Manganese . . . . . **9 %**
Vitamin B1 . . . . . **2 %**		

OTHER BENEFICIAL NUTRIENTS (PER SERVING)

Omega-3 (ALA) . . . . **60 mg**

TOMATO VELVET SOUP

6 CUPS • PREPARATION: 10 MINUTES • COOKING: 25 MINUTES • DIFFICULT

This is Andrew's goddaughter Devyn's absolute favorite soup! Not only is it delicious, but it is also rich in vital nutrients, such as lutein and vitamin C. I make the roux with gluten-free garbanzo-bean flour for a hearty, healthier flavor. Regular flour can always be used in any recipe; however, we love the nutty taste of garbanzo-bean flour and keeping it gluten-free.

1 tbsp olive oil

1 medium red onion, chopped

3 cloves garlic, minced

1 pack (10 oz) cherry tomatoes, washed and halved

1 can (14.5 oz) diced tomatoes

2 tbsp tomato concentrate

1 tsp agave nectar (optional)

Pinch each of salt and pepper

2 cups water or chicken broth

1 pack (2/3 oz) fresh basil

1 tbsp butter

2 tbsp garbanzo-bean flour

2 tbsp heavy whipping cream

1 In a large pot over medium heat, add olive oil and sauté the onion and garlic 2 or 3 minutes until the onion is translucent.

2 Add all the tomatoes (both fresh and canned) and tomato concentrate, agave, salt and pepper (to taste), water or broth and bring to a boil. Reduce heat to low and simmer for 15 minutes until the tomatoes are mushy.

3 In a blender, purée the soup until smooth.

4 In the same pot used earlier, make a roux over a low heat by melting butter and stirring in the garbanzo flour for a minute with a wooden spoon. Switch to a whisk and slowly add the whipping cream mixing until smooth.

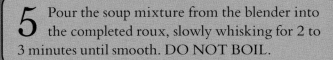

5 Pour the soup mixture from the blender into the completed roux, slowly whisking for 2 to 3 minutes until smooth. DO NOT BOIL.

6 Ladle into individual bowls, garnishing with fresh basil.

Nutrition Information

Serving Size **1 Cup**		Servings **6**
Calories **98**		Potassium . . . . . **432 mg**
Calories from fat . . **56**		Total Carbohydrates . **9 g**
Total Fat . . . . **6 g**		Dietary Fiber . . . . . **2 g**
Cholesterol . . . . . **12 mg**		Sugars . . . . **5 g**
Sodium . . . . **132 mg**		Protein . . . . **3 g**

Vitamin A . . . . **27 %**	Vitamin B1. . . . . **4 %**	Phosphorus. . . . . **5 %**
Vitamin C . . . . **39 %**	Vitamin B2. . . . **3 %**	Magnesium. . . . . **5 %**
Calcium . . . . **3 %**	Niacin . . . . **6 %**	Zinc . . . . **2 %**
Iron . . . . **4 %**	Vitamin B6. . . . **8 %**	Selenium . . . . . . **1 %**
Vitamin D3 . . . . **1 %**	Folic Acid. . . . . **6 %**	Copper. . . . . **7 %**
Vitamin E. . . . . . **7 %**	Vitamin B12. . . . **1 %**	Manganese . . . . **13 %**
Vitamin K . . . . **30 %**	Pantothenic Acid. **2 %**	

OTHER BENEFICIAL NUTRIENTS (PER SERVING)

Lycopene.	**3625 mcg**
Omega-3 (ALA)	**67 mg**
Choline.	**13 mg**
Beta-Carotene.	**380 mcg**
Lutein & Zeaxanthin.	**230 mcg**

CARROT, GINGER, TURMERIC AND COCONUT SOUP

6 – 8 CUPS • PREPARATION: 20 MINUTES • COOKING: 20 MINUTES • MEDIUM

One of our richer and higher calorie soups, it contains turmeric and ginger, which are at the top of the list of Andrew's favorite spices because they are so rich in protective health-promoting compounds. Coconut milk adds extra creaminess to this lovely soup.

1 tbsp coconut oil

1 tsp Asian Sesame oil

1 small red-hot chili pepper, seeded and chopped

3 tsp fresh ginger, peeled and grated

4 cloves of garlic, crushed

1 medium yellow onion, chopped

1 bag (12 oz) mini carrots, sliced

1 tsp cumin

1 tsp turmeric

1 can (13.5 oz) coconut milk

3 cups vegetable or chicken broth

Salt and pepper to taste

1/4 cup scallions, chopped

1 In a saucepan or wok over medium heat, warm the coconut and sesame oils. Add chili pepper, garlic and ginger sautéing 1 minute until aromatic. Add onion, carrots, cumin and turmeric sautéing an additional 2 minutes.

2 Pour in the coconut milk and broth, and bring to a boil. Reduce heat to low and simmer 13 to 15 minutes until carrots are soft and tender. Add salt and pepper to taste.

3 Working in batches, add soup into a food processor or blender on low speed until smooth. (I prefer using the blender because it makes the mixture much smoother.)

4 Pour into individual bowls garnishing with sliced carrots or chopped scallions.

Nutrition Information

Serving Size **1 Cup**   Servings **8**

Calories **200**	Potassium . . . . . **350 mg**	
Calories from fat . . **150**	Total Carbohydrates **11 g**	
Total Fat . . . . . . **17 g**	Dietary Fiber . . . . . **2 g**	
Cholesterol . . . . . . **3 mg**	Sugars . . . . **2 g**	
Sodium . . . . **70 mg**	Protein . . . . **3 g**	

Vitamin A . . . **180 %**	Vitamin B2 . . . . . **6 %**	Phosphorus . . . . **17 %**
Vitamin C . . . . **38 %**	Niacin . . . . **18 %**	Magnesium . . . . **11 %**
Calcium . . . . **5 %**	Vitamin B6 . . . . . **8 %**	Zinc . . . . **6 %**
Iron . . . . **18 %**	Folic Acid . . . . **11 %**	Selenium . . . . . . **6 %**
Vitamin E . . . . . . **2 %**	Vitamin B12 . . . . **5 %**	Copper . . . . **17 %**
Vitamin K . . . . **15 %**	Pantothenic Acid **3 %**	Manganese . . . . **42 %**
Vitamin B1 . . . . . **5 %**		

OTHER BENEFICIAL NUTRIENTS (PER SERVING)

Beta-Carotene	**2700 mcg**
Alpha-Carotene	**1600 mcg**
Lutein & Zeaxanthin	**220 mcg**
Choline	**8 mg**
Omega-3 (ALA)	**23 mg**

CREAMY CAULIFLOWER "DU BARRY" SOUP

8 – 10 CUPS • PREPARATION: 10 MINUTES • COOKING: 30 MINUTES • MEDIUM

This delicious soup makes it easy to enjoy the health benefits of cruciferous vegetables. I call it "du Barry," since anything made with cauliflower in France is referred to as "du Barry" after the French King Louis XV's mistress by the name of Madame du Barry who adored cauliflower.

1 tsp virgin coconut oil

1 garlic clove, minced

1 medium red onion, finely chopped

1 leek, washed and chopped (about 1 cup)

4 cups chicken broth

1 whole cauliflower, washed and broken into florets

1 tsp nutmeg

2 egg yolks

1 tbsp coconut flour

2/3 cup coconut milk

Salt and pepper to taste

3 sprigs fresh sage (for garnish)

1 In a large pot over medium heat, melt the coconut oil, and add garlic, leek and onion sautéing for 3 minutes until aromatic.

2 Add the broth and cauliflower, and bring to a boil. Add nutmeg, reduce heat and simmer for 20 minutes.

3 In a small bowl, whisk together egg yolks and coconut flour into a roux for thickening. Slowly add coconut milk.

4 In a blender, purée the hot soup mixture working in small batches until smooth. Blend in the egg yolk and coconut roux. Add salt and pepper to taste.

5 In the original soup pot over medium heat, add the blended mixture and cook for 2 minutes stirring constantly. DO NOT BOIL to avoid curdling.

6 Ladle the soup into individual bowls garnishing with fresh sage.

Nutrition Information

Serving Size **1 Cup**   Servings **10**

Calories **100**	Potassium . . . . . **320 mg**	
Calories from fat . . **60**	Total Carbohydrates . **7 g**	
Total Fat . . . . **7 g**	Dietary Fiber . . . . . **2 g**	
Cholesterol . . . . **45 mg**	Sugars . . . . **1 g**	
Sodium . . . . **50 mg**	Protein . . . . **3 g**	

Vitamin A . . . . . **2 %**	Vitamin B1. . . . . **4 %**	Phosphorus. . . . **13 %**
Vitamin C . . . . **48 %**	Vitamin B2. . . . . **6 %**	Magnesium. . . . . **6 %**
Calcium . . . . **3 %**	Niacin . . . . **14 %**	Zinc . . . . **4 %**
Iron . . . . **8 %**	Vitamin B6. . . . . **5 %**	Selenium . . . . . . **7 %**
Vitamin D3 . . . **1 %**	Folic Acid. . . . . **6 %**	Copper. . . . . . . **10 %**
Vitamin E. . . . . . **1 %**	Vitamin B12. . . . **5 %**	Manganese . . . . **24 %**
Vitamin K . . . . **10 %**	Pantothenic Acid. **6 %**	

OTHER BENEFICIAL NUTRIENTS (PER SERVING)

Lutein & Zeaxanthin.	**200 mcg**
Beta-Carotene.	**92 mcg**
Choline.	**35 mg**
Omega-3 (ALA)	**30 mg**

SWEET POTATO SPICE SOUP

10 - 12 CUPS • PREPARATION: 30 MINUTES • COOKING: 25 MINUTES • DIFFICULT

I love and enjoy sweet potatoes today, but they were not available when I was growing up in France. I first encountered them when I was 12 years old while reading Margaret Mitchell's book "Gone with the Wind;" but, I had to wait more than a decade to try them here in America.

3 tbsp coconut oil

2 medium brown onions, 1 chopped; 1 minced and reserved for garnish

2 cloves garlic, peeled and minced

1 tsp Garam Masala Indian spice mix

½ tsp turmeric

1 tsp cumin

1 tsp coriander

4¼ cups chicken broth

2 cups water

4 sweet potatoes, peeled and cubed

Salt and pepper to taste

1/3 cup coconut milk

Cinnamon cream Garnish (optional)

1 cup heavy whipping cream

1 tsp cinnamon

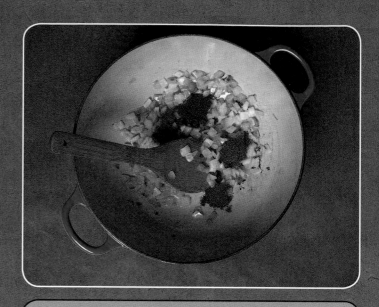

1 In a large pot over medium heat, warm half the coconut oil and sauté one of the onions and the garlic until the onion is translucent.

2 Add the Garam Masala, turmeric, cumin and coriander stirring constantly for 3 minutes until aromatic.

3 Add the chicken broth, water and sweet potatoes, and bring to a boil. Reduce heat and simmer for 15 minutes until sweet potatoes are tender. After simmering, add the coconut milk. Add salt and pepper to taste.

4 In a separate small pan over medium heat, warm the remaining coconut oil and sauté the remaining onion for 7 minutes until golden and crisp. Set aside for later.

5 Purée the soup in a food processor or blender, working in small batches if needed and blending until smooth.

6 In a medium bowl, whisk the whipping cream with the cinnamon for 5 minutes. Serve in individual bowls garnished with cinnamon cream and minced onion. (Optional)

Nutrition Information

Serving Size 1 Cup   **Servings 12**

Calories **86**	Potassium . . . . . **250 mg**	
Calories from fat . . **35**	Total Carbohydrates **11 g**	
Total Fat . . . . **4 g**	Dietary Fiber . . . . . **2 g**	
Cholesterol . . . . . . **0 mg**	Sugars . . . . **3 g**	
Sodium . . . . **151 mg**	Protein . . . . **2 g**	

Vitamin A . . . **123 %**	Vitamin B2. . . . . **2 %**	Phosphorus. . . . **4 %**
Vitamin C . . . . **14 %**	Niacin . . . . **3 %**	Magnesium. . . . . **4 %**
Calcium . . . . **3 %**	Vitamin B6. . . . . **6 %**	Zinc . . . . **2 %**
Iron . . . . **4 %**	Folic Acid. . . . . . **2 %**	Selenium . . . . . **1 %**
Vitamin E. . . . . . **1 %**	Vitamin B12. . . . **1 %**	Copper. . . . . **5 %**
Vitamin K . . . . . **1 %**	Pantothenic Acid. **4 %**	Manganese . . . . **11 %**
Vitamin B1. . . . . **3 %**		

OTHER BENEFICIAL NUTRIENTS (PER SERVING)

Omega-3 (ALA)	**2.8 mg**
Choline.	**7 mg**
Beta-Carotene.	**3680 mcg**

BUTTERNUT SQUASH SOUP WITH APPLE AND CURRY

6 - 8 CUPS • PREPARATION: 20 MINUTES • COOKING: 70 MINUTES • MEDIUM

This rich, delicious soup uses three of Andrew's favorite protective spices: cinnamon, nutmeg and curry. It is a rich source of protein, fiber and protective phytonutrients. We got the idea for our version of this soup from our friend Carrie who is the mother of Andrew's goddaughter.

1 butternut squash cut in half — approximately 1½ to 2 lbs

1 tbsp coconut oil

1 medium red onion (10 oz)

2 cloves of garlic

1 medium apple (6 oz), peeled and sliced

4 cups chicken broth

1 tbsp of curry powder

1 tsp cinnamon

1 tsp ground nutmeg

Pinch of salt and pepper

1/4 cup pecan halves, sautéed

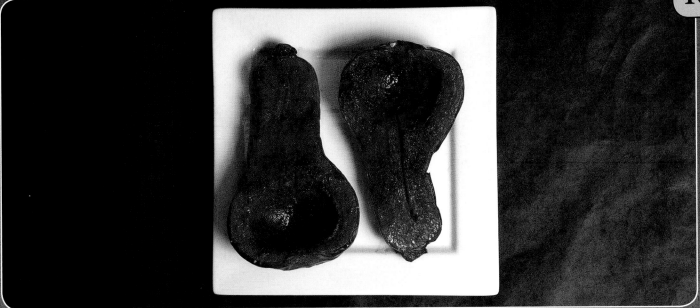

1 Preheat oven to 400. Sprinkle each half of the squash with half of the cinnamon and half of the nutmeg. Roast for 45 minutes. Let cool and scoop out the flesh.

2 In a 4- to 6-quart stock pot over medium heat, melt the coconut oil and sauté the onion, garlic and apple for 5 minutes.

3 Add broth, curry powder, the remaining cinnamon and nutmeg, and squash, and bring to a boil. Reduce heat to low and simmer for 20 minutes. Add salt and pepper to taste.

4 Purée in a blender or food processor working in small batches until smooth.

5 Serve in individual bowls with sautéed pecans sprinkled on top.

Nutrition Information

Serving Size 1 Cup   Servings **8**

Calories **115**	Potassium . . . . . . **600 mg**	
Calories from fat . . . **40**	Total Carbohydrates . **15 g**	
Total Fat . . . . **5 g**	Dietary Fiber . . . . . . **5 g**	
Cholesterol . . . . **3 mg**	Sugars . . . . **3 g**	
Sodium . . . . **50 mg**	Protein . . . . **3 g**	

Vitamin A . . . **150 %**	Vitamin B2 . . . . . . **6 %**	Phosphorus . . . . **14 %**
Vitamin C . . . **30 %**	Niacin . . . . **21 %**	Magnesium . . . **12 %**
Calcium . . . . **8 %**	Vitamin B6 . . . . **11 %**	Zinc . . . . **5 %**
Iron . . . . **9 %**	Folic Acid . . . . . . **8 %**	Selenium . . . . . **6 %**
Vitamin E . . . . . . **2 %**	Vitamin B12 . . . . **9 %**	Copper . . . . **14 %**
Vitamin K . . . . . **3 %**	Pantothenic Acid **6 %**	Manganese . . . . **36 %**
Vitamin B1 . . . . . **9 %**		

OTHER BENEFICIAL NUTRIENTS (PER SERVING)

Beta-Carotene	**3600 mcg**
Alpha-Carotene	**700 mcg**
Gamma Tocopherol	**2 mg**
Omega-3 (ALA)	**30 mg**

CREAMY ASPARAGUS SOUP WITH CHICKEN

7 – 8 CUPS • PREPARATION: 15 MINUTES • COOKING: 20 MINUTES • DIFFICULT

This is among Andrew's favorites because he loves the taste, but also because it is rich in protein, while ultra-low in calories and extremely rich in protective phytonutrients. Plus, it is a creamy soup with no added cream! The addition of chicken to traditional cream of asparagus soup hails from Portugal. I use gluten-free garbanzo-bean flour for the roux for a heartier taste.

2 bunches (about 1½ lb) asparagus

4¼ cups chicken broth

Pinch each of salt and pepper

1 tsp butter

1 tbsp garbanzo bean flour

2 tbsp milk

1 medium (approx. ½ lb) chicken breast

6 fresh sprigs of parsley for garnish

1 Prepare the asparagus: Cut off the heads of the asparagus (while retaining the rest of the asparagus stem), blanch the asparagus heads for 2 minutes in boiling salt water. Strain the asparagus heads and immediately plunge them in cold (ice) water to retard cooking. Strain and set aside.

2 In a 4-quart pot add the chicken broth to the asparagus stems cut in pieces. Bring to a boil and cook for 10 minutes or until asparagus is tender. Add salt and pepper to taste.

3 While the asparagus stems are cooking, sauté the chicken in a pan for about 7 to 10 minutes until done. Mince and set aside. Pour the soup mixture of asparagus stems into a blender or food processor, blending until smooth. Set aside.

4 In the same saucepan used for the soup mixture, melt butter adding the garbanzo bean flour and whisking until smooth and warm. Continue whisking while slowly adding the milk until well blended.

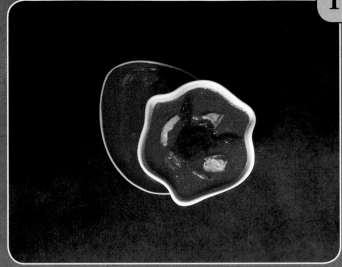

5 Slowly add to the garbanzo flour roux the puréed asparagus whisking until smooth and creamy. DO NOT BOIL. Add the minced chicken and cook for 3 minutes until the meat is warm.

6 Ladle into individual bowls garnishing with the asparagus heads and fresh parsley.

Nutrition Information

Serving Size Servings

Calories **77**	Potassium . . . . . **343 mg**
Calories from fat . . **15**	Total Carbohydrates . **4 g**
Total Fat . . . . **2 g**	Dietary Fiber . . . . . **2 g**
Cholesterol . . . . . **25 mg**	Sugars . . . . **2 g**
Sodium . . . . **212 mg**	Protein . . . . **12 g**

Vitamin A	**13 %**	Vitamin B2. . . .	**10 %**	Phosphorus. . . .	**13 %**
Vitamin C	**22 %**	Niacin	**26 %**	Magnesium.	**5 %**
Calcium	**4 %**	Vitamin B6. . . .	**13 %**	Zinc	**6 %**
Iron	**13 %**	Folic Acid.	**11 %**	Selenium	**14 %**
Vitamin E.	**5 %**	Vitamin B12. . . .	**3 %**	Copper.	**10 %**
Vitamin K	**44 %**	Pantothenic Acid.	**5 %**	Manganese	**10 %**
Vitamin B1.	**9 %**				

OTHER BENEFICIAL NUTRIENTS (PER SERVING)

Omega-3 (ALA)	**31 mg**
Choline.	**38 mg**
Beta-Carotene.	**419 mcg**
Lutein & Zeaxanthin.	**3680 mcg**

DELICIOUS, MINTY, COLD CUCUMBER SOUP

6 CUPS • PREPARATION: 10 MINUTES • CHILL TIME: 1 HOUR • VERY EASY

When I was learning how to cook, I spent time with a talented chef, Charles Dales in Aspen, Colorado, who was well known for his delicious cucumber/mint soup. Charles added caviar and sour cream; but, my version is simpler, healthier and more affordable without the caviar. At only 20 calories per serving this soup is the very definition of light and refreshing.

3 or 4 large cucumbers, seeded, peeled and chopped (approximately 2 lbs)

1 cup 2% Greek yogurt (reserve ½ cup for garnish)

2 cups water

Juice of one lemon

2 shallots, chopped

1 pack (2/3 oz) fresh mint

½ clove garlic

Pinch of cayenne pepper

Pinch each of salt and pepper

Garnish:

Fresh mint, a few leaves

½ tsp paprika

1 In a food processor or blender at low speed add cucumbers, yogurt, water, lemon, shallots, mint and garlic working in batches until mixture is smooth. Stir in salt, pepper and cayenne. Refrigerate for 1 hour.

2 Serve in individual bowls stirring in 1 tsp yogurt to each bowl for a creamier soup (optional). Garnish with fresh mint and sprinkled paprika (optional).

Nutrition Information

Serving Size **1 Cup**   Servings **6**

Calories **20**	Potassium . . . . . . **60 mg**
Calories from fat . . . **0**	Total Carbohydrates . **2 g**
Total Fat . . . . **0 g**	Dietary Fiber . . . . . **1 g**
Cholesterol . . . . . . **0 mg**	Sugars . . . . **2 g**
Sodium . . . . **15 mg**	Protein . . . . **2 g**

Vitamin A . . . . . **3 %**	Vitamin B1. . . . . **2 %**	Pantothenic Acid. **2 %**
Vitamin C . . . . . **6 %**	Vitamin B2. . . . . **3 %**	Phosphorus. . . . . **4 %**
Calcium . . . . **3 %**	Niacin . . . . **1 %**	Magnesium. . . . . **3 %**
Iron . . . . **1 %**	Vitamin B6. . . . . **3 %**	Zinc . . . . **2 %**
Vitamin E. . . . . . **1 %**	Folic Acid. . . . . . **3 %**	Copper. . . . . **3 %**
Vitamin K . . . . . **6 %**	Vitamin B12. . . . **1 %**	Manganese . . . . . **3 %**

OTHER BENEFICIAL NUTRIENTS (PER SERVING)

Beta-Carotene. . . . . **160 mcg**
Lutein & Zeaxanthin. . . . . **100 mcg**
Choline. . . . . **5 mg**

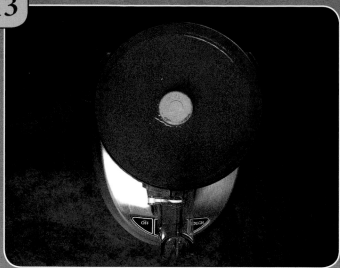

3 Add tomato concentrate, olive oil, vinegar, salt and pepper. Process until thoroughly mixed. Add salt and pepper to taste. Pour into a large bowl and refrigerate for at least 1 hour, but no more than 10 hours.

4 Serve in bowls or soup plates, garnishing with chopped onion, cucumber and pepper.

Nutrition Information

Serving Size **1 Cup**   Servings **10**

Calories **90**	Potassium . . . . . **380 mg**	
Calories from fat . . **45**	Total Carbohydrates . **9 g**	
Total Fat . . . . **5 g**	Dietary Fiber . . . . . **2 g**	
Cholesterol . . . . . . **0 mg**	Sugars . . . . **1 g**	
Sodium . . . . **20 mg**	Protein . . . . **2 g**	

Vitamin A . . . . **78 %**	Vitamin B1. . . . . **5 %**	Phosphorus. . . . . **3 %**
Vitamin C . . . **158 %**	Vitamin B2. . . . . **2 %**	Magnesium. . . . . **4 %**
Calcium . . . . . . **4 %**	Niacin . . . . . . **3 %**	Zinc . . . . **2 %**
Iron . . . . **3 %**	Vitamin B6. . . . **9 %**	Selenium . . . . . . **1 %**
Vitamin E. . . . . . **5 %**	Folic Acid. . . . . **8 %**	Copper. . . . . **5 %**
Vitamin K . . . . **10 %**	Pantothenic Acid. **2 %**	Manganese . . . . . **7 %**

OTHER BENEFICIAL NUTRIENTS (PER SERVING)

Lycopene.	**1418 mcg**
Beta-Carotene.	**1438 mcg**
Alpha-Carotene	**62 mcg**
Lutein & Zeaxanthin.	**86 mcg**
Choline.	**8 mg**
Omega-3 (ALA)	**27 mg**

Cold Avocado and Crab Soup

6 - 7 CUPS • PREPARATION: 10 MINUTES • CHILLING: 1 HOUR • VERY EASY

This is a lovely and rich soup (a bit higher in calories); but, still a healthy source of Omega-3s, protein and other nutrients. Rinse the crab meat before serving as it can otherwise be salty. Don't put paprika in the food processor because it can change the color of your soup. You can add it at the end and sprinkle it on top of the crab. It will look pretty and your soup will keep its bright green color.

4 large ripe avocados - halved, pitted and skinned

3 cups cold water

3 tbsp heavy whipping cream

Pinch of salt

1 tbsp agave nectar

Pinch of cayenne pepper (optional)

1 tsp white vinegar

1 tbsp fresh lime juice

Garnish

1½ cup fresh crab

½ tsp paprika

1 In a food processor, purée the avocado with the water, cream, salt, agave, cayenne pepper, vinegar and lime juice. Purée until smooth and creamy.

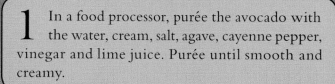

2 Serve immediately in chilled bowls, or cover with plastic wrap and chill for an hour or more. (The lime will stop it from getting brownish.) Garnish with Crab meat and paprika sprinkled on the top.

Nutrition Information

Serving Size **1 Cup**   Servings **7**

Calories **240**	Potassium . . . . . **610 mg**	
Calories from fat . . **165**	Total Carbohydrates **10 g**	
Total Fat . . . . **19 g**	Dietary Fiber . . . . . **7 g**	
Cholesterol . . . . . **35 mg**	Sugars . . . . **2 g**	
Sodium . . . . **100 mg**	Protein . . . . **9 g**	

Vitamin A . . . . **12 %**	Vitamin B1 . . . . . **7 %**	Phosphorus . . . . **12 %**
Vitamin C . . . . **19 %**	Vitamin B2 . . . . **10 %**	Magnesium . . . . **10 %**
Calcium . . . . **5 %**	Niacin . . . . **15 %**	Zinc . . . . **12 %**
Iron . . . . **5 %**	Vitamin B6 . . . . **19 %**	Selenium . . . . . **15 %**
Vitamin D3 . . . **2 %**	Folic Acid . . . . . **26 %**	Copper . . . . **17 %**
Vitamin E . . . . . . **9 %**	Vitamin B12 . . **5 %**	Manganese . . . . **10 %**
Vitamin K . . . . **33 %**	Pantothenic Acid **17 %**	

OTHER BENEFICIAL NUTRIENTS (PER SERVING)

Choline	**69 mg**
DHA	**43 mg**
EPA	**65 mg**
Omega-3 (ALA)	**168 mg**

MANGO, RED CURRY, CHICKEN SOUP

12 CUPS • PREPARATION: 20 MINUTES • COOKING: 25-30 MINUTES • MEDIUM

My favorite soup — an interesting combination of a remarkably healthy fruit with the benefits of curry. I do not add any salt because of the fish sauce, which is already extremely salty. You can find fish sauce on the Internet or in the Ethnic food section of many supermarkets.

1 tbsp sesame oil

1 medium red onion, chopped

2 tbsp Thai red curry paste

1 medium orange (or yellow) pepper, cut into small pieces

2 chicken breasts (about 1 lb), cut into small pieces

1 can (about 14 oz) coconut milk

4 cups chicken broth

2 ripe mangos, peeled and cubed

2 tbsp fish sauce

1 tbsp agave nectar, or honey

1 tbsp lime juice

1 tsp red chili pepper flakes (optional)

1 pack (2/3 oz) fresh basil leaves, minced (Thai basil recommended, but regular basil can be substituted)

GREEN CURRY THAI SOUP WITH SHRIMP

10 – 12 CUPS • PREPARATION: 20 MINUTES • COOKING: 25 MINUTES • MEDIUM

Most people think that curries are only red or yellow; but, there is a wonderful variety of green curry from Thailand that is extremely healthy and best of all – delicious! You will be surprised by the unique flavor it imparts to this recipe.

1 tbsp dark sesame oil

1 medium yellow onion (7 oz), chopped

2 tbsp green curry paste

2 cloves garlic, minced

2 tbsp fresh ginger, minced

1 tbsp lemon grass, minced

1 butternut squash (approx. 1 lb) cut in uniform small squares for even cooking

4 cups chicken broth

1 can (13.5 oz) coconut milk

1 tbsp fish sauce

½ tsp red–hot chili pepper flakes (spice to taste)

1 lb uncooked medium shrimp (approximately 22), peeled and deveined

5 fresh minced scallions

1 In a large wok over medium heat, warm sesame oil and sauté onion, curry paste, garlic, ginger and lemon grass stirring regularly for 5 minutes until aromatic.

2 Add squash, broth, coconut milk and fish sauce, and simmer for 15 minutes or until squash is cooked.

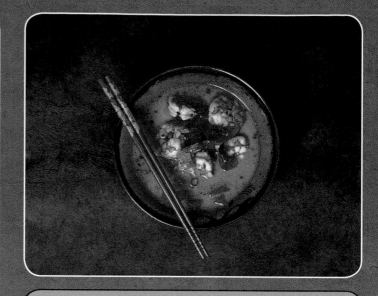

3 Add chili pepper flakes and shrimp cooking for an additional 3 to 5 minutes until shrimp turns pink.

4 Serve in individual bowls garnished with fresh minced scallions.

Nutrition Information

Serving Size **1 Cup**　　　　　　　　　　Servings **12**

Calories **160**	Potassium . . . . . **220 mg**
Calories from fat . . **90**	Total Carbohydrates . **8 g**
Total Fat . . . . **10 g**	Dietary Fiber . . . . . **2 g**
Cholesterol . . . . . **60 mg**	Sugars . . . . **1 g**
Sodium . . . . **305 mg**	Protein . . . . **10 g**

Vitamin A . . . . **52 %**	Vitamin B1 . . . . **4 %**	Phosphorus . . . . **12 %**
Vitamin C . . . **15 %**	Vitamin B2 . . . . **4 %**	Magnesium . . . . **10 %**
Calcium . . . . . . **5 %**	Niacin . . . . . **13 %**	Zinc . . . . **4 %**
Iron . . . . **13 %**	Vitamin B6 . . . . **6 %**	Selenium . . . . **10 %**
Vitamin D3 . . . . **4 %**	Folic Acid . . . . . **6 %**	Copper . . . . . . **11 %**
Vitamin E . . . . . . **4 %**	Vitamin B12 . . . . **4 %**	Manganese . . . . **39 %**
Vitamin K . . . . **18 %**	Pantothenic Acid. **3 %**	

OTHER BENEFICIAL NUTRIENTS (PER SERVING)

Beta-Carotene.	**1655 mcg**
Alpha-Carotene	**315 mcg**
Lutein & Zeaxanthin.	**80 mcg**
Choline.	**30 mg**
Omega-3 (ALA)	**17 mg**
DHA.	**12 mg**
EPA.	**11 mg**

CORAL LENTIL SOUP WITH CINNAMON AND CUMIN

8 – 10 CUPS • PREPARATION: 10 MINUTES • COOKING: 35 MINUTES • EASY

This soup originates in Morocco with its lovely combination of cinnamon and cumin. Andrew and I love all different kinds of lentils since they are so incredibly rich in protein, fiber and protective phytonutrients. My favorites are the coral lentils!

1 tbsp coconut oil

1 medium yellow onion, chopped

1 large clove garlic, minced

1 tsp cumin

½ tsp cinnamon

1 cup coral lentils

1 can (14.5 oz) diced tomatoes in their juices

5 cups water

Pinch each of salt and pepper

1/3 cup coconut milk

Juice of 1 lime

Mint leaves (optional)

1 In a large saucepan over medium heat, warm the coconut oil and sauté the onion, garlic, cumin and cinnamon for 3 to 5 minutes until aromatic.

2 Mix in the lentils and tomatoes and gradually add the water, salt and pepper. Bring to a boil. Reduce heat to low and simmer for 30 minutes or until the lentils are perfectly cooked.

3 Remove from heat and stir in coconut milk and lime juice.

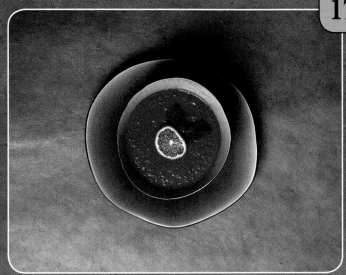

4 In a blender, blend well until smooth. Salt and pepper to taste.

5 Ladle into individual bowls, garnishing with lime slice and mint leaves.

Nutrition Information

Serving Size 1 Cup   **Servings 10**

Calories **105**		Potassium . . . . . **190 mg**
Calories from fat . . **30**		Total Carbohydrates **14 g**
Total Fat . . . . **3 g**		Dietary Fiber . . . . . **6 g**
Cholesterol . . . . . . **0 mg**		Sugars . . . . **2 g**
Sodium . . . . **70 mg**		Protein . . . . **6 g**

Vitamin A . . . . . **2 %**	Vitamin B1 . . . . . **4 %**	Phosphorus . . . . . **6 %**
Vitamin C . . . . **10 %**	Vitamin B2 . . . . . **2 %**	Magnesium . . . . . **4 %**
Calcium . . . . . . **2 %**	Niacin . . . . **3 %**	Zinc . . . . **2 %**
Iron . . . . **12 %**	Vitamin B6 . . . . . **5 %**	Selenium . . . . . . **2 %**
Vitamin E . . . . . **1 %**	Folic Acid . . . . . **11 %**	Copper . . . . **16 %**
Vitamin K . . . . . **2 %**	Pantothenic Acid . **5 %**	Manganese . . . . **21 %**

OTHER BENEFICIAL NUTRIENTS (PER SERVING)

Choline . . . . **20 mg**
Gamma Tocopherol . . . . **1 mg**
Omega-3 (ALA) . . . . **50 mg**
Lycopene . . . . **525 mcg**

3 Place the soup in a food processor or the blender for 1 or 2 minutes at low speed. Add spinach for a few seconds at low speed. You want to see cut leaves, not a purée.

4 Add lemon juice with additional salt and pepper to taste. Serve in individual bowls, garnishing with lemon slice and small spinach leaf.

Nutrition Information

Serving Size **1 Cup**   Servings **7**

Calories **130**	Potassium . . . . . **210 mg**
Calories from fat . . **20**	Total Carbohydrates **19 g**
Total Fat . . . . **2 g**	Dietary Fiber . . . . **10 g**
Cholesterol . . . . . . **0 mg**	Sugars . . . . **0 g**
Sodium . . . . **30 mg**	Protein . . . . **8 g**

Vitamin A . . . . **16 %**	Vitamin B1 . . . . . **5 %**	Phosphorus . . . . . **7 %**
Vitamin C . . . . . **8 %**	Vitamin B2 . . . . . **3 %**	Magnesium . . . . . **6 %**
Calcium . . . . **2 %**	Niacin . . . . **2 %**	Zinc . . . . **3 %**
Iron . . . . **15 %**	Vitamin B6 . . . . . **6 %**	Selenium . . . . . . **2 %**
Vitamin E . . . . . . **2 %**	Folic Acid . . . . . **18 %**	Copper . . . . **21 %**
Vitamin K . . . . **54 %**	Pantothenic Acid . **2 %**	Manganese . . . . **19 %**

OTHER BENEFICIAL NUTRIENTS (PER SERVING)

Lutein & Zeaxanthin	**1000 mcg**
Beta–Carotene	**480 mcg**
Choline	**160 mg**
Omega–3 (ALA)	**100 mg**

GREEN LENTIL AND VEGETABLE SOUP

9 - 11 CUPS • PREPARATION: 20 MINUTES • COOKING: 1 - 1 ½ HOURS • MEDIUM

The green French lentils in this soup make it exceptionally rich in protein, fiber and best of all, flavor. Green French lentils are not your typical lentils; but, they can be found on the Internet or at organic or specialty food stores. The small addition of tomato paste is an exceptional source of lycopene.

2 tbsp olive oil

1 medium yellow onion
   (7 – 8 oz), chopped

3 cloves garlic, minced

1 cup leeks, washed thoroughly
   and chopped

1 cup diced celery

1 cup diced carrots

1 tsp cumin

Pinch each of salt and ground
   pepper

1½ cups green French lentils

8 cups beef broth

1 pack (2/3 oz) fresh thyme
   (reserve 8 sprigs for garnish)

1 bay leaf

2 tbsp tomato paste

3 tbsp red wine

1 In a large pot over medium heat, warm the olive oil and sauté the onion, garlic, leek, celery, carrots, cumin, salt and pepper for 5 minutes until aromatic.

2 Add lentils, broth, thyme, bay leaf and tomato paste, and bring to a boil. Lower heat and simmer uncovered for 1 hour until everything is tender.

3 Stir in red wine and remove bay leaf.

4 Serve in individual bowls garnished with thyme sprigs.

Nutrition Information

Serving Size **1 Cup**　　　　　　　　Servings **11**

Calories **160**	Potassium . . . . . **340 mg**
Calories from fat . . **40**	Total Carbohydrates **20 g**
Total Fat . . . . **4 g**	Dietary Fiber . . . . **10 g**
Cholesterol . . . . . . **0 mg**	Sugars . . . . **3 g**
Sodium . . . . **235 mg**	Protein . . . . **10 g**

Vitamin A . . . . **45 %**	Vitamin B2 . . . . . **7 %**	Phosphorus . . . . **16 %**
Vitamin C . . . . **15 %**	Niacin . . . . **12 %**	Magnesium . . . . **12 %**
Calcium . . . . **6 %**	Vitamin B6 . . . . **12 %**	Zinc . . . . **10 %**
Iron . . . . **17 %**	Folic Acid . . . . **36 %**	Selenium . . . . . . **6 %**
Vitamin E . . . . . . **4 %**	Vitamin B12 . . . . **3 %**	Copper . . . . **9 %**
Vitamin K . . . . **15 %**	Pantothenic Acid **7 %**	Manganese . . . . **26 %**
Vitamin B1 . . . . **17 %**		

OTHER BENEFICIAL NUTRIENTS (PER SERVING)

Lycopene . . . . **830 mcg**
Beta-Carotene . . . . **1150 mcg**
Alpha-Carotene . . . . **400 mcg**
Lutein & Zeaxanthin . . . . **200 mcg**
Choline . . . . **36 mg**
Omega-3 (ALA) . . . . **65 mg**

BARLEY AND GREEN LENTIL SOUP WITH ITALIAN CHICKEN-SAUSAGE

5 - 6 CUPS • PREPARATION: 20 MINUTES • COOKING: 1⅓ HOURS • MEDIUM

This stew-like soup is absolutely wonderful, hearty and healthy. (The chicken and apple sausage is not always readily available in supermarkets depending on your locale. However, several varieties are available for order online.) As this soup is more like a stew, feel free to add 1 cup of water if you want it more "soup like."

2 tbsp olive oil

1 cup sliced leek

1 medium brown onion, chopped

2 cups vegetable broth

2 cups water

1 bottle of beer (I use Corona®)

1 cup chopped carrots

1 cup chopped celery

¼ cup chopped dill

¼ cup uncooked Barley

3 bay leaves

3 tsp of fresh thyme

½ cup lentils

4 Italian chicken sausages (about 10 oz) pricked with a fork to let in air

Salt and pepper to taste

1 In a medium-sized pot over medium heat, warm olive oil, and add the leek and onions sautéing for 3 minutes and stirring occasionally until vegetables are soft.

2 Stir broth, water and beer into the pot and bring to a boil.

3 Add carrots, celery, dill, barley, bay leaves and thyme, and return to a boil. Reduce heat and simmer for 15 minutes. Stir in the lentils, cover and cook on low for an additional 30 to 40 minutes.

4 While the soup is simmering, preheat a frying pan until hot adding the sausage and cooking 10 to 15 minutes until golden brown on all sides. You can first cut the sausage into small uniform pieces and then cook, if desired.

5 Remove the bay leaves from the soup, and add salt and pepper to taste.

6 Serve in individual bowls, topping with sausage pieces.

Nutrition Information

Serving Size **1 Cup**　　　　　　　　Servings **6**

Calories **280**	Potassium . . . . . . **360 mg**
Calories from fat . . **110**	Total Carbohydrates . **28 g**
Total Fat . . . . **12 g**	Dietary Fiber . . . . . . **8 g**
Cholesterol . . . . . . **50 mg**	Sugars . . . . **2 g**
Sodium . . . . **400 mg**	Protein . . . . **16 g**

Vitamin A . . . **126 %**	Vitamin B2. . . . **14 %**	Phosphorus. . . . **26 %**
Vitamin C . . . . **18 %**	Niacin . . . . **26 %**	Magnesium. . . . **18 %**
Calcium . . . . . **10 %**	Vitamin B6. . . . **24 %**	Zinc . . . . **20 %**
Iron . . . . **22 %**	Folic Acid. . . . . **42 %**	Selenium . . . . . **26 %**
Vitamin E. . . . . **10 %**	Vitamin B12. . . . **6 %**	Copper. . . . . . . **16 %**
Vitamin K . . . . **34 %**	Pantothenic Acid **8 %**	Manganese . . . . **38 %**
Vitamin B1. . . . **44 %**		

OTHER BENEFICIAL NUTRIENTS (PER SERVING)

Omega-3 (ALA)	**360 mg**
Choline.	**80 mg**
Total Tocotrienols	**9 mg**
Beta-Carotene.	**2000 mcg**
Alpha-Carotene	**740 mcg**
Lutein & Zeaxanthin.	**40 mcg**

PEARL BARLEY SOUP
WITH VEGETABLES

8 - 10 CUPS • PREPARATION: 15 MINUTES • COOKING: 1 HOUR • EASY

This is a nutritious meal in itself. To save time, soak the barley overnight or at least five hours prior to beginning soup preparations. It is a remarkable source of lutein, zeaxanthin, tocotrienols and more.

2 tsp olive oil

1 medium brown onion, chopped

1 clove garlic, minced

2 large carrots, chopped

1 leek, washed well and chopped

1 stalk celery, chopped

1 cup pearl barley (soaked overnight)

6 cups chicken broth

1 bay leaf

1 can (14.5 oz) fire-roasted tomatoes

3 cups fresh spinach, roughly chopped

Salt and pepper to taste

Fresh tarragon

1 In a large saucepan or stock pot over medium heat, warm olive oil and add onion, garlic, carrots, leek and celery cooking for 3 minutes until the onions become soft and translucent.

2 Add barley, broth and bay leaf. Reduce heat to medium low, cover and simmer for 50 minutes to an hour until barley is tender.

3 Stir in the tomatoes and spinach, salt and pepper to taste, and simmer for an additional 6 to 7 minutes.

4 Ladle soup into bowls and garnish with fresh tarragon.

Nutrition Information

Serving Size **1 Cup**		Servings **10**

Calories **130**		Potassium . . . . . **350 mg**
Calories from fat . . **30**		Total Carbohydrates **21 g**
Total Fat . . . . **3 g**		Dietary Fiber . . . . . **5 g**
Cholesterol . . . . . . **0 mg**		Sugars . . . . **3 g**
Sodium . . . . **110 mg**		Protein . . . . **5 g**

Vitamin A	**62 %**	Vitamin B2.	**5 %**	Phosphorus. . . .	**10 %**
Vitamin C	**30 %**	Niacin	**11 %**	Magnesium. . . .	**10 %**
Calcium	**5 %**	Vitamin B6.	**8 %**	Zinc	**5 %**
Iron	**11 %**	Folic Acid.	**10 %**	Selenium	**11 %**
Vitamin E.	**6 %**	Vitamin B12. . . .	**2 %**	Copper.	**11 %**
Vitamin K	**67 %**	Pantothenic Acid.	**2 %**	Manganese	**27 %**
Vitamin B1.	**6 %**				

OTHER BENEFICIAL NUTRIENTS (PER SERVING)

Omega-3 (ALA)	**58 mg**
Choline.	**16 mg**
Total Tocotrienols.	**21 mg**
Beta-Carotene.	**1630 mcg**
Alpha-Carotene	**420 mcg**
Lutein & Zeaxanthin.	**1350 mcg**
Lycopene.	**525 mcg**

GREEN SPLIT PEA SOUP

9 – 10 CUPS • PREPARATION: 15 MINUTES • COOKING: 1 – 1½ HOURS • MEDIUM

Andrew's favorite! It is a wonderfully creamy soup! Rinse the optional ham hock well before cooking as it can be very salty. I wait until the end to add salt to taste.

1½ cup dry split peas, rinsed

1 tbsp olive oil

1 medium yellow onion, chopped

1 clove garlic, minced

1 smoked ham hock (optional)

1 cup chopped carrots

2 medium stalks celery, chopped

4 cups chicken broth

4 cups water

6 thyme sprigs or 1 tsp dry thyme (reserve some for garnish)

1 bay leaf

Pinch each of salt and pepper

1 In a large saucepan or stock pot over medium heat, warm the olive oil and add onion, garlic and ham hock (optional), sautéing for 2 to 3 minutes until the onion is translucent.

2 Add carrots, celery, split peas, broth and water. Mix well and bring to a boil.

3 Add thyme and bay leaf. Lower heat and simmer for 1 to 1-1/4 hours stirring occasionally until all the ingredients are well cooked. Salt and pepper to taste.

4 Remove bay leaf and ham hock (optional) scraping the meat from the bone.

5 Working in small batches, mix soup into a blender at low speed until smooth.

6 Stir in the ham and ladle into individual bowls garnished with thyme sprigs.

Nutrition Information

Serving Size **1 Cup**   Servings **10**

Calories **130**	Potassium . . . . . **228 mg**
Calories from fat . .**20**	Total Carbohydrates **20 g**
Total Fat . . . . **2 g**	Dietary Fiber . . . . . **8 g**
Cholesterol . . . . . . **0 mg**	Sugars . . . . **2 g**
Sodium . . . . **40 mg**	Protein . . . . **7 g**

Vitamin A . . . . **47 %**	Vitamin B2. . . . **28 %**	Phosphorus. . . . **58 %**
Vitamin C . . . . **14 %**	Niacin . . . . . **1 %**	Magnesium. . . . **16 %**
Calcium . . . . **6 %**	Vitamin B6. . . . **46 %**	Zinc . . . . **56 %**
Iron . . . . **8 %**	Folic Acid. . . . . . **7 %**	Selenium . . . . . **82 %**
Vitamin E. . . . . . **6 %**	Vitamin B12. . . **26 %**	Copper. . . . . . . **22 %**
Vitamin K . . . . . **8 %**	Pantothenic Acid **19 %**	Manganese . . . . **14 %**
Vitamin B1. . . . **20 %**		

OTHER BENEFICIAL NUTRIENTS (PER SERVING)

Beta-Carotene.	**1100 mcg**
Alpha-Carotene	**445 mcg**
Choline.	**288 mg**
Omega-3 (ALA)	**68 mg**
Lutein & Zeaxanthin.	**55 mcg**

SPINACH AND CHICKPEA SOUP WITH LEMON

5 – 6 CUPS • PREPARATION: 10 MINUTES • COOKING: 30 MINUTES • VERY EASY

This hearty, healthy and nutritious soup is an exciting combination of ingredients originating in Portugal.

1 tbsp olive oil

1 medium red onion, chopped

2 cloves of garlic, minced

1 can (15 oz) chickpeas, drained

4 cups of chicken broth

1 tsp of cumin

1 package fresh spinach, roughly chopped

2 tbsp of fresh lemon juice

Salt and pepper to taste

1 In a large pot over medium heat, warm olive oil, and add the onion and garlic sautéing for 2 to 3 minutes until the onion is translucent. Add the chickpeas, broth and cumin, and bring to a boil. Reduce heat and simmer 15 minutes until the flavors are well blended.

2 Transfer soup to a food processor adding the spinach and pulsing a few times. This goes very quickly. You do not want to purée, but chop into small pieces.

3 Return the soup to the large pot cooking for an additional 5 to 7 minutes. Add lemon juice, salt and pepper to taste. Ladle into serving bowl garnishing with a slice of lemon.

Nutrition Information

Serving Size **1 Cup**   Servings **6**

Calories **162**	Potassium . . . . . **496 mg**
Calories from fat . . **38**	Total Carbohydrates **23 g**
Total Fat . . . . **4 g**	Dietary Fiber . . . . . **7 g**
Cholesterol . . . . . . **0 mg**	Sugars . . . . **4 g**
Sodium . . . . **200 mg**	Protein . . . . **9 g**

Vitamin A . . . . **44 %**	Vitamin B2. . . . . **7 %**	Phosphorus. . . . **16 %**
Vitamin C . . . . **37 %**	Niacin . . . . **7 %**	Magnesium. . . . **14 %**
Calcium . . . . **8 %**	Vitamin B6. . . . . **9 %**	Zinc. . . . . **9 %**
Iron . . . . **18 %**	Folic Acid. . . . . **42 %**	Selenium . . . . . . **4 %**
Vitamin E. . . . . . **5 %**	Vitamin B12. . . . **1 %**	Copper. . . . . . . **17 %**
Vitamin K . . . **146 %**	Pantothenic Acid. **3 %**	Manganese . . . . **53 %**
Vitamin B1. . . . . **8 %**		

OTHER BENEFICIAL NUTRIENTS (PER SERVING)

Omega-3 (ALA)	**82 mg**
Choline.	**36 mg**
Beta-Carotene.	**1330 mcg**
Lutein & Zeaxanthin.	**2880 mcg**

HEARTY TURKEY CHILI

13 - 14 CUPS • PREPARATION: 15 MINUTES • COOKING: 1 HOUR • EASY

This incredibly rich and hearty source of protein and fiber is Andrew's post-workout favorite. This wonderful chili can be made in advance and refrigerated up to two days. It is also delicious served over brown rice.

2 tbsp olive oil

1 medium red onion, chopped
(reserve a little for garnish)

1 cup chopped green pepper

1 cup chopped red pepper

4 garlic cloves, minced

1 tbsp cumin

1 tbsp red–hot chili pepper flakes

2 to 4 tbsp chili powder,
depending on heat preference

1 pack (10 oz) cherry tomatoes,
halved

1 can (14.5 oz) diced tomatoes

2 tbsp tomato paste

1 can (15 oz) kidney beans, rinsed

2 cans (15 oz ea.) black beans,
rinsed

1½ cups chicken broth

1 tsp dry oregano

4 cups ground or shredded
turkey meat, cooked

1 tbsp salt

1 pinch ground pepper

6 oz white Cheddar cheese,
shredded (optional)

1 cup Crème Fraiche (optional)

1 In a 4 to 6 quart soup pot over medium heat, warm olive oil and add onion and peppers, stirring until golden in color.

2 Add garlic, cumin, chili powder and red pepper flakes cooking for an additional 2 minutes.

3 Add tomatoes (both fresh and canned), tomato paste, broth, rinsed beans, oregano, turkey, salt and pepper, and bring to a boil. Reduce heat to low and simmer for an hour.

4 Ladle into individual bowls garnishing with shredded cheese and Crème Fraiche.

Nutrition Information

Serving Size **1 Cup**   Servings **14**

Calories **195**	Potassium . . . . . **265 mg**
Calories from fat . . **55**	Total Carbohydrates **22 g**
Total Fat . . . . **6 g**	Dietary Fiber . . . . . **9 g**
Cholesterol . . . . . **26 mg**	Sugars . . . . **2 g**
Sodium . . . . **110 mg**	Protein . . . . **13 g**

Vitamin A . . . . **22 %**	Vitamin B2. . . . **17 %**	Phosphorus. . . . . **9 %**
Vitamin C . . . . **89 %**	Niacin . . . . **19 %**	Magnesium. . . . **13 %**
Calcium . . . . . . **4 %**	Vitamin B6. . . . **17 %**	Zinc . . . . **11 %**
Iron . . . . **13 %**	Folic Acid. . . . **23 %**	Selenium . . . . . **12 %**
Vitamin E. . . . . . **6 %**	Vitamin B12. . . . **1 %**	Copper. . . . . . . **15 %**
Vitamin K . . . . **10 %**	Pantothenic Acid. **7 %**	Manganese . . . . **21 %**
Vitamin B1. . . . **23 %**		

OTHER BENEFICIAL NUTRIENTS (PER SERVING)

Omega-3 (ALA)	**221 mg**
Choline.	**25 mg**
Beta-Carotene.	**530 mcg**
Lutein & Zeaxanthin.	**123 mcg**
Lycopene.	**1550 mcg**

ANDREW'S FAMILY
"CURE ALL" CHICKEN STOCK

10 CUPS OR MORE • PREPARATION: 20 MINUTES • COOKING: 4 HOURS • MEDIUM

This recipe is originally from Andrew's grandmothers and goes back several generations. Andrew's mother and sister with whom I have a special relationship were so sweet to share it with me. It is delicious!

Notes: Andrew's sister does not add any garlic to her stock. However, you can if you wish. The quantity of this soup depends on the size of your stock pot. Because it is a stock (only liquid) you can make a lot at one time.

1 large, whole, organic chicken (about 4½ to 5 lb), divided into parts (neck, back, breast, wings etc.)

1 medium onion, chopped in 4 pieces

1 bag (1 lb) mini carrots

4 celery stalks, quartered

3 leeks, washed and cubed

4 sprigs fresh dill

4 sprigs parsley

2 bay leaves

3 sprigs fresh thyme

Pinch of Kosher salt

½ tsp black peppercorn

1 tomato, halved

1 In an 8-quart stock pot, combine the chicken parts, onion, carrots, celery and leeks. Add water until everything is covered by 2 inches. Heat over medium low heat for approximately 1 hour. Skim the top.

2 Bunch together the dill, parsley, thyme and bay leaves, and tie with a string. Add to the stock pot along with the salt, black peppercorn and tomato. Cover and simmer on low 2 to 3 hours (longer if you wish).

3 Strain and degrease. Remove the herbs and chicken.

4 You may wish to remove or leave the chicken and/or vegetables in the soup. Andrew's mother leaves all the vegetables and the chicken in the soup while his sister only leaves the carrots.

Nutrition Information

Serving Size **1 Cup**		Servings **10**
Calories **40**		Potassium . . . . . **206 mg**
Calories from fat . . .**9**		Total Carbohydrates . **3 g**
Total Fat . . . . **1 g**		Dietary Fiber . . . . . **0 g**
Cholesterol . . . . . . **0 mg**		Sugars . . . . **0 g**
Sodium . . . . **70 mg**		Protein . . . . **5 g**

Calcium . . . . . . **1 %**	Folic Acid. . . . . . **2 %**	Zinc. . . . . **3 %**
Iron . . . . **2 %**	Phosphorus. . . . . **4 %**	Selenium . . . . . . **5 %**
Niacin . . . . **16 %**	Magnesium. . . . . **2 %**	

INDEX

NOTES

NOTES

NOTES